Illustrator:
Howard Chaney

Editor:
Evan D. Forbes, M.S. Ed.

Editor in Chief:
Sharon Coan, M.S. Ed.

Art Director:
Elayne Roberts

Assistant Art Coordinator:
Cheri Macoubrie Wilson

Cover Artist:
Karen Fong

Product Manager:
Phil Garcia

Imaging:
Evan D. Forbes, M.S. Ed.

Publishers:
Rachelle Cracchiolo, M.S. Ed.
Mary Dupuy Smith, M.S. Ed.

INTERNET FOR KIDS

Primary

Author:

Sandy Spaulding

Teacher Created Materials, Inc.
P.O. Box 1040
Huntington Beach, CA   92647
ISBN-1-55734-187-4

©1998 Teacher Created Materials, Inc.   Made in U.S.A.

TABLE OF CONTENTS

INTRODUCTION

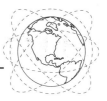

"So much to do and so little time"—this is the familiar lament of teachers worldwide.

And that is counting just the numbers of books, paper, and pencils that are used daily, not accounting for the other numerous consumers of time.

Well, rev up your adventurous spirit and hang on to your hat! With this hands-on tour of the Internet, we are about to glide (not zoom) through a universe of knowledge that reduces student essays, even whole textbooks, to mere blips on the screen or, if you will, clicks on the mouse.

And do you know what? Even if you complete every one of this book's activities, you and your students will only have scratched the surface of the Internet.

That vastness is part of the fun and challenge of teaching with the Internet.

Notice, though, that I say *teaching* with the Internet. The Internet is a tool, a resource, an enhancement to the all-important job you perform every day.

This book is a tool as well as just a little something to reinforce what you are already doing in your classroom or the lab or even at home.

How to Use This Book

Internet for Kids is not meant to be a comprehensive look at the Internet. This book will leave that to those books that are so large you can read their titles at a hundred paces. In this book, you will be given some of the basics of connecting with the seemingly unlimited, always-changing Internet's educational resources. For starters, here are . . .

The Basics of the Basics

Hardware you will need:

1. PCs that are 386 or faster or 68030 Macs or Power Macs—the faster, the better

2. A computer with at least eight megabytes of RAM (random access memory) and a 250-megabyte or larger hard disk (You can get by with less.)

3. A modem with a speed of at least 14,400 bits per second

Tools you will need for full Internet access:

1. E-mail software (At this time, Pegasus and Eudora Light can be downloaded free from the Internet.)

2. Newsreader software (This manager enables you to access Usenet news groups.)

3. File-transfer-protocol client software (ftp)

4. Gopher client software

5. Telnet software

6. World Wide Web browser (Your browser has probably incorporated tools 1–5.)

7. TCP/IP software. This provides your basic connection to the Net and is usually provided by your ISP (Internet Service Provider).

* A very helpful addition, if your school has the funds, is some kind of projection system that will allow for more full-class demonstrations and browsing.

INTRODUCTION *(cont.)*

Before moving on to the activities, there are a few points I'd like to cover.

1. Integrate the Internet into your curriculum and time line by choosing activities that coordinate with your lessons. As for time, my goal is to get students to their destinations as quickly as possible.

2. We all need something to show for our efforts. Therefore, most of these activities have a worksheet. Modify them to best fit your students' style and yours. Many of these pages are designed to be bound into class books.

3. There are a few basic assumptions that I have made in writing this book:

   • You have access to a computer that is connected to the Internet and World Wide Web.

   • You have a basic ability to navigate through your operating system (Microsoft Windows or Macintosh OS.)

As a teacher and author, I am counting on you, the reader, to understand a few things.

   • IMPROVISE. If an activity looks like it may not work for your students, but you like the basic idea, modify the end product. As a teacher, you pick and choose and modify lessons as the day progresses. Working with students on the Internet is no different.

   • The activities in this book can be completed by a single student in a lab setting, in cooperative groups, or in a single computer in the classroom. Use the grouping that works best for you.

   • If you have only one connected computer in the room, have a dependable student or adult work with the students completing the activity.

   • Training one or two students to be your "Computer Wizards" will free up your time immensely.

   • Please read the section on copyright laws. The misuse and abuse of copyrighted materials on the Internet has become a hotly debated issue. If you have questions on copyrights and the Internet, check the bibliography for more resources.

   • Avoid any problems with students, parents, and the school board. Make sure your school district and site have an Acceptable Use Policy in place. I discuss this topic and provide samples later in the book.

The most often used services and capabilities of the Internet are broken down and discussed in the beginning of this book. Most of these tools are easily accessible on the Web with a quick point and click of the mouse. Therefore, the activities included in the book are primarily Web-based, although ftp, gopher, newsgroups, and mailing lists are still Internet services.

A personal note regarding newsgroups, mailing lists, and chat rooms—I have found that these services can be fun to monitor. However, even on the education-specific lists I have been hard pressed to find information that I would want to use. You may find these services useful, but personally, I spent a great deal of time reading and clearing out e-mail messages.

COPYRIGHT CONCERNS

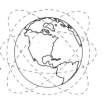

Because the Internet is a somewhat new medium in the public's hands, there are several gray areas surrounding copyright. However, "Gee, your honor! There are so many gray areas!" is no defense if someone ever chooses to sue you or your school for playing fast and loose with intellectual property.

By the time you read this, there should be some clearer guidelines on copyright, but in case there are not, here are some that might help (with assistance from the founder of ClariNet, Brad Templeton, and his *Ten Big Myths About Copyright Explained*).

---

1. Almost everything is copyrighted the minute it is written. No copyright notice is required.

2. As much as possible, your students should paraphrase and give attribution. (That is solid writing practice anyway.)

3. Whether you charge money or not, you can still violate someone's copyright.

4. E-mail and material posted in newsgroups and on bulletin boards are still protected. Whether you or other authors want to make an issue out of protected material is for another forum.

5. What about fair use? This is a concept/term schools often turn to for guidance. Basically, keep it short and give attribution. Use only what is necessary to make your point.

6. Do not assume that by using others' material that you are helping to promote original work. The author may, in fact, appreciate it, but he/she will appreciate it more if you ask permission. Besides, he/she may have valid reasons for not granting permission.

7. What about photographs, online graphics from Web pages, and drawings/diagrams? Elementary school students cannot always go around clipping pictures (including the credits) out of encyclopedias and the latest new magazines. On the up side, asking permission from Web sites is usually just a matter of sending a quick e-mail message and awaiting an equally quick response.

Connecting to the Net Via Commercial Services

Members of the two leading commercial online services—America Online (AOL) and Prodigy—need only a few mouse clicks to hop directly onto the Internet.

On America Online, clicking the Internet Connection button on the main menu will take members to the various Net services, including their own World Wide Web browser.

ELECTRONIC MAIL

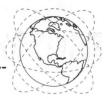

Electronic mail may well be your first completed task on the Internet. If you have your teacher-friend Bill Smith's Internet address (it might look like this: bsmith@aol.com), you can send him messages that will reach him almost instantly, even if he is in Hawaii and you are in Boston. For him to reply to you, he generally needs to simply click the mouse button or tap a key and start typing. When he is through with his reply, it is a matter of another mouse click and off it goes.

Teachers: Do your students have to type all their messages on the same computer? No. If they have a PC at home or elsewhere in the school, they can type their messages, save them on a floppy as text (a generic version of unformatted, word-processed copy that almost any computer can read), and then copy/paste them into your e-mail program on the connected computer.

Let us take a quick look at Bill Smith's Internet address, also known as his e-mail address: **bsmith@aol.com**
user name   bsmith (Bill Smith)
@
organization name   aol   (America Online)
organization type   com   (commercial)

Some E-Mail Bits:

1. Try to read and respond to e-mail while you are offline so you do not tie up the phone line as well as waste money. Most e-mail programs will read and store copy quickly so you can sign off and peruse it at your leisure.

2. If you receive a message that you want to share with another teacher, there is usually a button to forward the same message to another recipient. There will also be a box to type in a quick message to that new recipient.

3. By using the carbon copy feature, you can scatter the same message to several recipients. Just make sure that you correctly type their e-mail addresses.

4. As with all of your writing, keep your audience in mind. Friends will be more tolerant of ramblings, while acquaintances will probably want you to get to the crux of your message as quickly as possible.

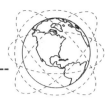

5. Again, depending upon your audience, keep your messages factual to avoid any misunderstandings. After all, e-mail is basically words on a screen with very little context attached—no facial expressions, no body language, no tone of voice.

6. If you share the electronic mailbox with other teachers, ask your correspondents to include your name on the subject line. It lets others know whom the mail is for, thus offering some semblance of privacy.

7. If you are new to e-mail, practice sending e-mail to yourself, just to get the fundamentals down. Once you are comfortable with that, find a friend who is an e-mail veteran and correspond for a day or two.

8. Here is a realistic scenario: Fred e-mailed you yesterday, and it is on your to do list to write back. Rather than reply from scratch, dig into your in box, find the original message, and click the reply command. Why? (1) Most e-mail software automatically includes the original message in your reply. That way, you can make sure you refer to all issues addressed. (2) By keeping pertinent info from that first message, you are reminding the recipient what issue you are discussing.

9. Do not underestimate the helpfulness of an informative subject line. When pressed for time, readers need to know what they must read now and what they can leave for later. If you want a fairly immediate response, words like "a question for you" hardly evoke action. Instead, squeeze in your question, such as, "Want an extra VCR?"

10. It can be easy to confuse someone's e-mail address with a Web site's address. For example, Bill Smith may be a contributor at a Web site (http://www.teamteachers.org/), but he takes his personal e-mail at bsmith@aol.com. The two addresses yield very different resources.

Classroom Uses of E-Mail

- Make that first contact to collaborate with other classes.
- Share science data with another class.
- Become pen pals (also known as key pals) with other classes.
- Keep up-to-date with other teachers in the middle of collaborative projects.
- Exchange student book reviews.
- Trade banter/commiserate/exchange teaching tips with colleagues.
- Set up an interclass debate on a subject of your choice.
- Challenge a partner class with math word problems.
- Read the same literature book as another class and team up on related activities.
- Subscribe to educational mailing lists, such as Connect with KIDLINK. (http://www.kidlink.org)

MAILING LISTS

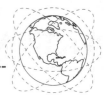

I was perusing newsgroup postings from new users, and many of the subject headings were of the "send me some e-mail" ilk. I wondered if some of these users had not yet discovered mailing lists (also known, semi-accurately, as listservs). If you want e-mail, this is the corner of the Net to explore.

Focused on specific topics, mailing lists might also be called "e-mail clubs." Subscribe to one that interests you, and you will soon be receiving members' messages that are broadcast (by one main computer, called the listserv, list processor, or majordomo, depending on the software used) to all other list members. In other words, send your message to the listserv, and your words will be sent automatically to the other subscribers.

Where Do You Find These Mailing Lists?

To get a list of current viable mailing lists, look up Publicly Accessible Mailing Lists (by Stephanie Da Silva) in the Usenet groups news.lists and news.answers, or using a Web search engine, try the keywords: listserves educational.

For a shortcut to education-related mailing lists, refer to my list below or point your Web browser to EdWeb (http:k12.cnidr.org/). Once you find a mailing list that catches your eye, click on its name, and you will connect to an e-mail form that will let you subscribe right there.

An active list can net you 50 or more messages a day. At my school, I joined KIDSPHERE, and by day's end, we had over 20 messages awaiting our attention. They all had meaningful content. (Depending on the list you select, this may or may not be the case.)

Keep in mind, then, that reading (or even deciding to delete without reading) several messages takes time, so be ready for that minor intrusion into your computer time. When your eyes are blurry and you have lost interest in the list, feel free to unsubscribe.

To subscribe to a mailing list from your own e-mail program, this is what you do:

If you want to subscribe to KIDSPHERE, e-mail them at the following address:

kidsphere-request@vms.cis.pitt.edu

In the body of the message, type the words:

subscribe KIDSPHERE John Smith

(substituting your own first and last names for John Smith).

To unsubscribe, simply substitute the word unsubscribe for subscribe in the above example.

Note: Do not worry if you get it wrong the first time. The list's computer will send your request back with a hint of what you need to do when you try again. Use common sense, read your frequently-asked-questions files, and you will be all right.

Your first piece of mail from the list will be a welcome message and a set of instructions on how best to communicate with the list, including posting messages and sending requests. Copy and paste those instructions into a text file for future reference.

Mailing List Bits:

- Some mailing lists are moderated (screened by people), while others are unmoderated (the mail is passed along as is).

- Keep the introductory information sent by the list administrator. It offers guidelines on subscribing, unsubscribing, posting messages, sending requests, etc.

- When you receive a message that you wish to respond to, ask yourself:

  — Will my response be of interest to just the sender? If so, double-check the sender's e-mail address and respond to him/her only.

  — Will my response further a group discussion or offer value to most members of the list? If so, send your message to the entire group.

- When you subscribe or unsubscribe, make sure you are sending that request to (again, depending on the list manager software) the listserv, the listproc, or the majordomo, not to the group.

- See if your list administrators offer a DIGEST option. It keeps your mailbox manageable by accumulating the postings and sending them to you in one file on a weekly basis.

- If you are going to be gone for a length of time, you can temporarily stop delivery. (Just today, a KIDSPHERE subscriber had over 248 messages awaiting him upon his return from vacation.)

Classroom Uses of Mailing Lists

- Advertise your own interclass projects.

- Remain current with curricular areas. (Simply look up and subscribe to a list that focuses on whatever is the current interest of your class.)

- Glean teaching ideas from other educators.

- Find out about the latest interclass projects.

Here are a few education-related mailing lists you might consider; they are followed by the e-mail address.

1. BILINGUE-L—developmental bilingual elementary education list, listserv@Reynolds.k12.or.us
2. CHATBACK—special education discussion, listserv@sjuvm.stjohns.edu
3. EDTECH—education and technology list, listserv@msu.edu
4. EKIDS—Electronic Kids Internet Server list, majordomo@citybeach.wa.edu.au
5. KIDCAFE—kids' discussion group, listserv@vm1.nodak.edu
6. KIDLINK—information on KIDS-95, listserv@vm1.nodak.edu
7. KIDS-ACT—activity projects for kids, listserv@vm1.nodak.edu
8. KIDSPHERE—international KIDLINK discussion, kidsphere@vms.cis.pitt.edu
9. MULTIAGE—multiple-age schooling list, listproc@services.dese.state.mo.us
10. WWWEDU—The World Wide Web in Education, listproc@educom.unc.edu

USENET NEWS

If you want news with a major slant, a chance to air your opinions, information galore on hobbies, umpteen ways to connect with other teachers, or just plain silliness, subscribe to Usenet newsgroups.

Accessing Usenet news is really pretty simple. You have newsreader software (the software that reaches a Usenet server, which serves up the latest postings for subscribers to read). Use it to . . .

> . . . view the newsgroups available to you.
>
> . . . subscribe/unsubscribe to newsgroups from that list.
>
> . . . peruse a list of the articles' headings.
>
> . . . click on and read the ones that interest you.
>
> . . . respond to those postings that spark the writer in you.

There are two categories of newsgroups: standard and alternative. Among the standard newsgroups, there are seven main hierarchies:

- comp (computers)
- news (Usenet itself)
- rec (sports, hobbies, recreation)
- sci (science)
- soc (social issues)
- talk (unmoderated discussion on controversial topics)
- misc (miscellaneous)

As a teacher who has to answer for the content to which your students are exposed, keep close tabs on any newsgroups you join. You are fairly safe with most education-related groups, but you are never completely protected from brainless interlopers. It will not hurt to read the postings for a couple of days before you choose to include your students.

Usenet Bits:

1. After subscribing to a newsgroup, be sure to read its FAQs (frequently asked questions). Doing so will prevent you from posing questions that have already been asked. Plus, you will learn more about that group's subject.

2. Lurk for about a week after joining. In other words, take time to read the postings to get acquainted with the group's focus, nuances, and expectations. (You can learn a lot from others' mistakes along the way.)

3. Do not do test messages to see if you are actually subscribed. Odds are you will get flamed (verbally assailed online) for contributing a meaningless message to the group's discussions.

4. Take the time to learn your newsreader program. There will be some buttons whose functions may not be immediately clear. A mistake here can be embarrassing for you and aggravating to the newsgroup.

5. If a posting arouses your ire or admiration on a personal level, you might want to e-mail its author rather than share that emotion with the whole group. Just let your common sense take over.

USENET NEWS *(cont.)*

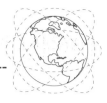

Usenet Bits: *(cont.)*

6. DO NOT TYPE IN CAPITAL LETTERS! It is interpreted by others as shouting. HEY! YOU IN THE BACK! ARE YOU LISTENING?

7. When responding to a posting, try to quote the pertinent excerpt to keep your comments in proper context. Most newsreader software will let you quote the previous posting.

Classroom Uses of Usenet News

- Find people with varying views on curriculum-related subjects.
- Find people knowledgeable on curriculum-related subjects.
- Advertise for collaboration on Net projects.
- Connect with teachers (see groups below) with all kinds of interests.
- Stay up-to-date on conferences, new projects, software, contests, and grants.
- Access large collections of freeware and shareware.

How to Find Newsgroups

Following is a fairly comprehensive list of education-related newsgroups. (See below.) Most Web browsers should send you to a newsgroup when you type "news:" followed by a group's name into the location indicator (the narrow text box where URLs appear) and then press enter. A subscribe option should be available at the bottom of the page.

You can always use a Web search engine and type in the keyword Usenet. The various hits (references that include the keyword) should lead you to plenty of selections, most of which you can click on, read, and subscribe to.

- misc.education—discussion of the educational system
- misc.education.home-school.misc—almost anything about homeschooling
- misc.education.language.english—teaching English to speakers of other languages
- misc.education.multimedia—multimedia for education (moderated)
- misc.education.science—issues related to science education
- alt.education.disabled—learning experiences for the disabled
- alt.education.distance—learning over nets, etc.
- alt.education.email-project—the e-mail project for teaching English
- k12.ed.soc-studies—social studies and history curriculum in K–12 education
- k12.ed.special—K–12 education for students with handicaps or special needs
- k12.ed.tag—education for talented and gifted students
- schl.sig.k12admin—K–12 school administrators
- clari.nb.education—computers in education
- comp.edu—computer-science education
- comp.edu.composition—writing instruction in computer-based classrooms
- schl.news.edupage—Educom's thrice-weekly EDUPAGE Newsletter

CHATS ON THE NET

As you might expect, chatting is talking online. While future technologies will enable more and more users to easily hear and even see each other (see section on video), for most of us, chatting is simply exchanging typed text that you and your fellow conversationalists can read on the screen.

Things can get a little confusing if there are several parties involved, such as when the spoken words which appear on the screen do not necessarily follow a cohesive pattern. But a little experience goes a long way in keeping up with the flow of conversation. So, just take your time and remember with whom you are talking.

Not counting techno-heaven, where two communicating classes use high-speed fiber optic cabling to teleconference, here are some of your main choices to chat through your computer.

1. Chat Rooms on Commercial Services

When it comes to ease of use, I prefer this option. On America Online, for example, my classes have chatted with ecologists in Georgia and a partner class in a Geography Detectives project. The real highlight, though, was our friendship with Frank, our retired key pal/chat partner in Long Island. With Frank, we observed Veterans Day by asking him questions about his World War II experiences in Europe. (This brought a sometimes obscure holiday much closer to kids' consciousness.) During the Christmas season, we hopped back into the chat room to exchange Christmas traditions and memories. It was nice to have my West Coast students get a taste of an old-time Christmas in Frank's childhood home in a snow-laden forest. These vivid experiences, while possible otherwise, would not have been as instantaneous and effective without today's chat capabilities.

How do you do this? Just set up a date and time with your partner(s). AOL's Electronic Schoolhouse provides its own chat room, or you can create your own in that service's main chat facility.

2. The Internet Relay Chat

For teachers, Internet Relay Chat is certainly a viable option, but it does require a few extra steps. You will need to . . .

- . . . use a separate piece of software to use IRC. Ircle for the Mac and mIRC and Wsirc for PCs are three such programs.
- . . . learn commands to effectively converse online.
- . . . sift for a channel (chat group) that focuses on your intended subject matter and whose participants behave appropriately for your students. You do have the option to set up your own personal channel and then invite your own chat partners.

Because the learning curve for IRC is not necessarily high, it may not be worth your while, considering most teachers' time constraints.

IRC, does, however, include KIDLINK (http://www.kidlink.org), which offers countless learning possibilities, including its own IRC for kids.

3. Web Chat Sites

During a night of Web browsing, I found a site dedicated to homeschooling, along with activities such as Collaborative Calculator and kid-organized links to other home-ed resources.

This home page provided two chat rooms—one for students and one for the parent-teachers. There was a box for your typed comments, a button to send them, and a button to update the chat (i.e., see your partners' latest remarks).

4. Explore the World of MUD

MUDs (multi-user dimensions) have taken on a variety of forms. If you are familiar with interactive adventure games, such as Zork, you basically know what MUDs are. Generally, users construct and interact with text-based environments. Perhaps something of more interest to you in this genre is the MOO (MUD-Object Oriented), which places more emphasis on an environment's objects. Users can chat and interact with other characters in a physical environment, including rooms and furniture.

If you want to tailor one to your class's needs, you will want to . . .

> . . . become comfortable with Telnet, an Internet service that allows you to connect to another computer and use its resources.

> . . . become completely comfortable with the basic commands.

> . . . learn as much about MOO as possible—how many sites your students can visit and what makes each site special.

> . . . make sure your choice of MOO allows for a whole class.

> . . . find one that initially allows for more chat and less creation while you become comfortable with the other participants.

Another variation on the multi-user theme is the MUSE (multi-user simulation environment). Massachusetts Institute of Technology's Artificial Intelligence Lab has created MicroMuse, which offers some of the most intriguing examples in this genre. MicroMuse highlights include the following:

- MicroMuse Science Center features interactive exhibits from science museums across the country.
- Mission to Mars is highlighted by a virtual tour of the fourth planet from the sun. This is not just a strap-yourself-in-and-sightsee trip, either. You must team up with other users and navigate your way to the Red Planet.
- Narnia Adventure challenges users with puzzles related to this C.S. Lewis classic. As with most of these environments, the puzzles require, or at least inspire, collaboration.

To connect to MicroMuse:

1. Telnet to: 128.89.2.137
2. Log in as: guest
3. Type: connect guest
4. Type: look (to look at surroundings)
5. Or go to the Micro Muse Website at gopher://cyberion.

The following are some MUD-related Internet sites:

MUD Resource (http://www.godlike.com/muds)

Jason Nolan's MOO projects and an experimental MOO (http://www.oise.on.ca/~jnolan/moo.html)

Traci Gardner's MOO Tip Sheet for Teachers (http://www.daedalus.com/net/MOOTIPS.html)

Chat Bits:

- To ensure your comments are clearly intended for a specific person, precede your words with that person's screen name.
- Ideally, you should have some kind of large-screen setup so your whole class can follow along.

VIDEO ON THE NET

While live video chats are not yet a daily happening at most schools, the technology is there to make it possible, even affordable. Outside of schools, in fact, CU-SeeMe (one software application, thanks to Cornell University, that makes video-conferences possible) is being used in clubs to broadcast live music performances and in so-called Cyber Cafes for those who want to hang out with people across the country.

If you are interested in video chats at your school, you will need the following:

- a modem that offers a connection of 28.8 bps or faster (Some people have held chats at a speed of 14.4 bps.)
- an IP connection to the Internet or direct Ethernet connection, ISDN, dial-up SLIP, or PPP
- a computer that can display 16-level grayscale (i.e., most color PCs or Macs)
- a $100 Connectix QuickCam or, at a higher cost, a camcorder with NTSC 1 vpp output
- software that makes the class-to-class connection possible (CU-SeeMe does this)
- video digitizing software (if you are sending video)
- a connection to a reflector site if you want to conference with more than one other computer *(See below.)

*For Windows users, the Connectix VideoPhone is a $150 software solution for those often required tweaks and system adjustments.

Currently, you can download a version free from its Web site—http://cu-seeme.cornell.edu. If you want the commercial version, technical support, purchasing options, etc., you can purchase it from White Pine Software.

I used CU-SeeMe to receive video with my 28.8 modem. (You do not need the QuickCam to receive.) I was impressed, not necessarily by the quality of the video, which can be erratic, but by the fact that these people's live images were being flashed on my computer screen and I was actually having an audio conversation.

Here is a sample video chat that could occur between two classes using CU-SeeMe software.

The two connected groups should take the following steps:

- For a two-party conference, choose Connect from the Connection menu. Type in the partner's IP address.
- For a multiparty conference, enter the IP address of a reflector. (See below.)
- Check the local video window (the one that shows the image they are sending) and use on-screen controls to sharpen brightness and contrast and adjust the transmission rate for no more than 80 kilobytes per second and the transmission resolution to standard. High resolution places much greater demands on a normal phone line connection (ISDN or T-1 users could probably use high resolution). Audio options, some of which may not be available, depend upon the computer's operating system.
- Check the Input Window. (This shows the partners' images.) Under this window are control buttons that do the following:
  1. tell whether partners are accepting sound and/or video images at the moment.
  2. allow you to control the volume of incoming sound.

- Connect with a reflector site if more than two groups are connecting. (Currently there are over 60 reflector sites, with more popping up daily.)

Both groups may also choose to type their comments back and forth.

What will they see and hear? Maybe smooth, flowing images or maybe jerky, several-frames-a-second images and often garbled voices, but somehow the fact that they are seeing and hearing their partners live should keep them conversing.

Video Bits:

- Give users what they are looking for, live video. For some reason, some users leave the room but stay connected or send still shots. If you are not going to be at the controls, it is better to sign off and leave the band width for someone else.

- If you are at a busy reflector site, try to lower your transmission rate. An acceptable rate is 50 kilobits per second.

- Do you have questions? Point your browser to http://cu-seeme.cornell.edu or http://www.jungle.com/msattler/sci-tech/comp/CU-SeeMe/. Both sites are very helpful.

- Here is a list of Public Reflectors (Digital Conference Bridges):

Organization	Reflector IP#	Contact person	e-mail address
NYSERNET	192.77.173.2	Jean Armour Polly	jpolly@nysernet.org
CORNELL	192.35.82.96	Dick Cogger	r.cogger@cornell.edu
PENN	130.91.72.36	Dan Updegrove	updegrove@dccs.upenn.edu
CNIDR	128.109.178.103	Jane Dunlap Smith	jds@kudzu.cnidr.org
QMS	161.33.3.1	James Hill	jamesh@qms.com
GTE	132.197.10.74	Alan R. Bugos	abugos@gte.com
Norway	158.36.33.3	Barre Ludvigsen	borrel@dhhalden.no
HAWAII U	128.171.171.10	Craig Miller	cvmiller@uhunix.uhcc.hawaii.edu

Site 1   **Site 2**

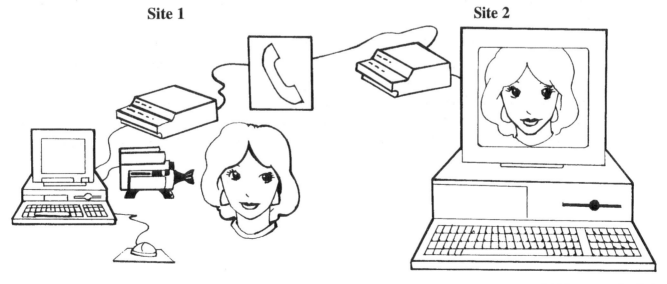

FILE TRANSFER PROTOCOL

File transfer protocol, FTP, opens up a world of computer files of all types for you to download (transfer) as long as you follow a few steps.

There are several ways to FTP files. Let us discuss the three most efficient.

1. You can use an Archie client, a piece of software that connects you to FTP sites and searches through their files.

2. Simply type its URL in your Web browser's location indicator and press enter.

3. Visit ArchiePlex, a World Wide Web-based Archie gateway by Martijn Koster. This site lets you enter a keyword, and the software does the work.

Once we reach a FTP site, many of us just browse and download what we think is useful. If you do not have the time or luxury to browse and download, you need to know two things:

1. the file's name. (Here is an example: whale.qt stands for a *Quicktime* file of a whale.)

2. the type of file it is so you can use the correct retrieval mode, binary for non-text files and text for text-based files.

FTP Bits:

1. Always scan your newly downloaded files with antivirus software.

2. Keep an eye on available space on your hard drive. The ease with which you can download files can quickly lead to a full hard drive.

3. GIF directories (often appearing as folders) will provide images.

4. Other useful directories are named /pub/MSdos for PC users and /Mac for Mac users.

5. To save connect time, many FTP files are compressed when transferred. You will need software utilities such as *Stuffit* (Mac), *BinHex* (Mac), or *Pkunzip* (PC) to decompress them.

6. Most of the time you will be using a method called anonymous FTP. This means that you are able to access the files as a guest. In fact, guest is usually the word you type when you are asked to log in. If the FTP site asks for your password, your full e-mail address will usually suffice. (Keep in mind that most FTP client software takes care of these steps.)

Classroom Uses of FTP

1. FTP sites provide large numbers of information and graphics files.

2. You can download helper applications to add capabilities to your Web browser.

3. You can get software updates almost as soon as they are released.

SAMPLE FTP SESSION

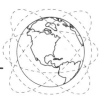

In this search, I tried to play the role of someone fairly new to file transfer protocol (FTP), or at least someone just knowledgeable enough to be dangerous. My discussion of FTP will give you more direct routes to utilizing this resource. At times, you will run across the "user anonymous access denied" message. Do not worry about this; there are plenty of other sites to search for the same file.

1. I went to Yahoo (an Internet search engine), looked through the main index, and chose "Computers and Internet."

2. I clicked on the listing of subcategories.

3. I clicked on Archie.

4. I chose one of the Archie gateways offered.

The server is either busy or not accepting queries at this time.

(During a school day, there is often heavy use of some of the resources you are trying to access. You should always have a backup ready.)

5. I tried another gateway which took my search for whales to a site in Norway. Normally, it is considered good "netiquette" to stay with sites close to home. However, since all the U.S. sites I had tried were busy, I traveled overseas.

Search used eight seconds and gave 52 hits. **Note:** You have to like the speed of this search. Can you imagine looking through a catalog and finding 52 potentially helpful references in just eight seconds?

Here is a sampling of the files that were referred:

WHALE.AVI (a video file)	Aug 25 13:45	(11777326 bytes)
whale.GIF (an image file)	Jan 13 18:50	(589 bytes)
whale.GIF (an image file)	Jan 13 18:50	(79050 bytes)
whale.dat (accumulated data)	Dec 19 20:52	(94483 bytes)
whale.dat (accumulated data)	May 11 1993	(94483 bytes)
whale.qt (a video file)	Sep 1 21:53	(11727970 bytes)

6. I followed the link below and got an abundance of data on whales. However, much of it I could not understand.

whale.dat (accumulated data)	Dec 19 20:52	(94483 bytes)

7. My next link:

whalenet	Mar 3 1994	(3159 bytes)

The following is a sampling from a two-page document:
Broaden Your Whale Watch Horizons
WhaleNet, in conjunction with the Whale Conservation
Institute (WCI) and whale watch companies, is developing a
program to enhance the educational use of whale watches.
WhaleNet offers curriculum support and a source of data
for interdisciplinary classroom activities and interactive
informational support for students through the EnviroNet bulletin boards utilizing
telecommunications.

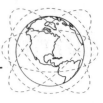

8. Yet another link follows:

   Whale.gif   Dec 21 18:50   (1953 bytes)

It was a nice little postage-stamp-sized image.

9. I quit Netscape and started up Anarchie, which is Archie client software for the Macintosh. It led me to a multitude of sites and bookmarks.

10. I went to a mirror site of the University of Michigan's FTP site. A mirror site contains the same files as another more popular site. It is set up to distribute activity to more than one site.

11. Under the File menu, I selected Archie and entered whale as my search word. I pressed return and it started its search. It told me that the search would last 15 minutes, but it actually lasted only about a minute.

12. I saved a bookmark for Anarchie, called whale bookmark. I will try it later.

13. As I was nearing my 30-minute time limit, I downloaded an 86-card HyperCard stack on whales and signed off.

GOPHER

Gopher—1. a furry little rodent-pest that digs efficiently toward its culinary destinations and, in the process, brings gardeners to their knees and infuriates golf course officials 2. official mascot of the University of Minnesota

Gopher—a very efficient Internet research tool, developed at the University of Minnesota, that allows users to dig efficient linear paths to information

As a research tool, Gopher does not offer the glitz, glamour, or flexibility of the World Wide Web, but, as noted in the above definition, it is efficient. It lets you dig down through directories of information and lets you dig back up to retrace your path. Gopher servers are accessed primarily via the Web, Gopher client software, or a Telnet connection.

Gopher Bits:

- Get to know Veronica (Very Easy Rodent-Oriented Net Indexed Computerized Archives), a Gopher utility which, with the assistance of your entered keyword (typed-in search term), searches through almost every Gopher server in the world to find related documents.

- To access Gopher from the Web, just type the server's URL into the location indicator and press enter/return.

- Visiting the Web site for Gopher Jewels (http://galaxy.einet.net/GJ/index.html) is another way to reach Gopher servers.

- Consider using Gopher client software, such as TurboGopher for the Mac and WinGopher for the PC. These applications will allow you to bypass the Web connection and tunnel straight to Gopher sites.

- What kinds of files can you access?

    — text files (which you can view on screen)

    — graphics files (which you can also view on screen with the right software)

    — binary files (which you can download on the spot)

    — indexes that can lead you on a narrower search

SAMPLE GOPHER SESSION

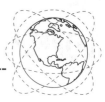

I spent 30 minutes searching Gopherspace for information on whales. This was one of my first times to do a Gopher search. The next time, it will take even less time.

- When I use italics, I am quoting some of what appeared on the screen during my search.

- You will see that not every document was helpful, but I did not waste too much time finding that out.

- The score that follows the listed document is the server's way of telling you how directly that reference matches your keyword. (For the most part, the higher the score, the better the chance you will gain helpful information.)

1. I entered the following URL (for Gopher Jewels) into Netscape's location indicator: http://galaxy.einet.net/gopher/gopher.html. Gopher Jewels is a nifty little tool that searches a large number of helpful Gopher servers. Their searches first yield titles of documents and other searchable directories (seen on screen as folders).

2. I entered whales as my search keyword.

3. I read over the search results for "whales, finding":

59 documents; 159 more qualifying matches remain.

The Gopher server also told me I could use Boolean phrases (such as, and, or, and not) to refine my search. (For example, entering "whales, not dolphins" would limit the results to just whales.)

4. When I looked up the document below, I was told the server returned no data. For this session, then, I reached a dead end. But, I can always try another server.

Document #1: 83.02.12: Dolphins and Whales in Mythology: Part One of a Multidisciplinary Unit—Score: 1000

5. I tried this document next and came up with the information on a free teaching kit.

Document #2 Adopt a Whale—Score: 1000

For more information on adopting a whale or for a free teaching kit, contact:

The Whale Adoption Project, 634 North Falmouth Highway, P.O. Box 388, North Falmouth, MA 02556, or call (508)564-9980.

6. Another interesting hit was this one.

Document #3 Ancient Whale Walked on Land—Score: 1000

January 13, 1993

This was a United Press International story that certainly caught my attention. It said that, according to a report in the journal *Science,* at least one predecessor of the modern-day whale walked on land. This was based on a fossil discovery that was dated 52 million years old.

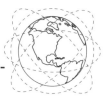

7. This was the next document. (You certainly do not have to follow the list in order. In my case, each reference was intriguing.)

Document #4 Whale of a Story—Score: 1000

I was refused a connection to the site that offered this story.

8. Upon learning yet another intriguing title, I tried to translate this file. I received an "end of file error" message.

Document #5 whale.bin 94-02-02- 3K—Score: 1000

9. I made a bookmark for this great Gopher search tool.

10. I left Netscape, and I tried another approach to Gopherspace—TurboGopher, a Macintosh application that started my search right at the University of Minnesota, where Gopher originated.

11. From TurboGopher's main menu, I selected "Other gopher and information servers."

12. This led me to VERONICA, another efficient Gopher search tool.

13. Once again, I entered "whales" into the keyword box.

14. I was refused at one site because it was too busy—too many connections. *Try again soon.* So I clicked on another site.

15. I downloaded a graphic of whales hunting. While this was downloading in the background, I was able to continue my search.

16. I downloaded a small software application called "whale." It turned out to be unrelated to whales. Such is the case when you try to decipher file names.

17. I hit a gold mine on baleen whales. But my self-imposed 30-minute time limit was up.

WORLD WIDE WEB

So much has already been written about the World Wide Web that I am going to try to say as little as possible but still share the Web's important functions.

The World Wide Web . . .

- . . . is based on millions of linked hypertext documents. Hypertext allows users to point and click (rather than type commands) to follow author-embedded links (found in many Web page graphics and virtually all of its underlined pieces of text).
- . . . requires browser software, such as Netscape Navigator and the various versions of Mosaic. Many other browsers are out there, all with their own strengths. Lynx, for example, is the most-used text-based browser, meaning it offers words, but not the graphics, that most other browsers do.
- . . . is the component that has thrust the Internet into the public's (and schools') consciousness.
- . . . is bursting into the classroom. In 1995, Web66, a leading clearinghouse of school home pages, witnessed a 1,249% increase in home pages entered in their registry.
- . . . provides teachers a better packaging of information than the other Net components, such as Gopher and FTP.
- . . . interacts quite efficiently with other Net components.
- . . . offers students many more opportunities to create, publish, design, and interact with the Net.
- . . . opens up even more opportunities for teachers to connect internationally.
- . . . can be accessed through the major commercial online services, as well as many local providers.
- . . . allows its millions of users to buy and sell products and services online.
- . . . opens up all kinds of information, both appropriate and inappropriate, to your students. (There are software programs, such as SurfWatch, that act as a kind of gatekeeper to let in the suitable information and keep out the unsavory material.)

Your Web Browser

The Internet software tool you will most utilize will be your Web browser.

Browser software should . . .

- . . . let you keep a list of favorite sites to visit, by means of a hotlist or bookmarks.
- . . . offer nearly seamless integration with other Internet components such as FTP, electronic mail, Gopher, and Usenet news.
- . . . make downloading of files a simple process.
- . . . let you easily retrace your current session's path (or history) through the sites you have visited (i.e., links you have followed).
- . . . work hand in hand with helper applications that facilitate your computer's handling of video, sound, and graphics.
- . . . make the creation of Web pages workable with a little guidance from books or tutorials.

The World Wide Web offers much more than you see above, but are a good starting point for any browser.

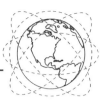

Edit: Edits current page on your screen only

Go: Lists sites you have visited this session; allows you to return from this screen

Bookmarks: Add bookmarks, edit your list

Options: Screen viewing and setup

Directory: Link to Netscape sights

Window: Screen viewing options

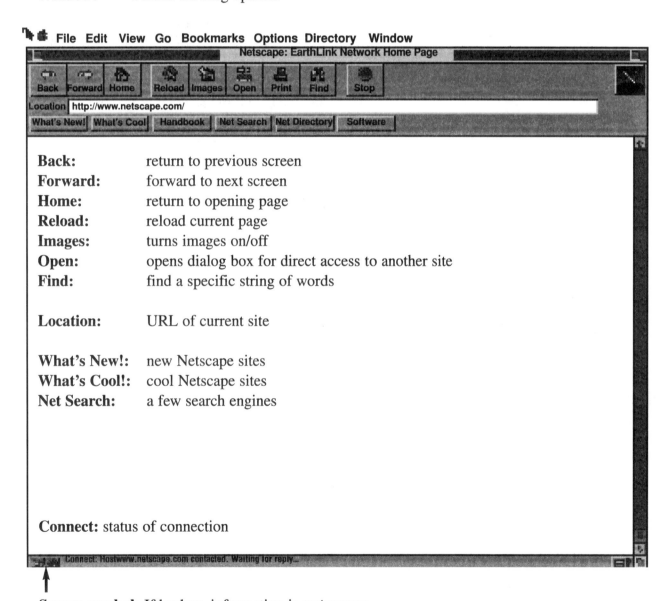

Back: return to previous screen
Forward: forward to next screen
Home: return to opening page
Reload: reload current page
Images: turns images on/off
Open: opens dialog box for direct access to another site
Find: find a specific string of words

Location: URL of current site

What's New!: new Netscape sites
What's Cool!: cool Netscape sites
Net Search: a few search engines

Connect: status of connection

Secure symbol: If broken, information is **not** secure.

(Netscape Communications, the Netscape Communications logo, Netscape, and Netscape Navigator are trademarks of Netscape Communications Corporation.)

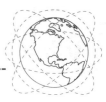

Web Bits:

- Have a clear idea of what you want from the Web. Otherwise, you will have wandered far and wide without finding nearly as much as you originally wanted.

- See if your Web browser lets you open multiple windows. If so, you can be downloading software in one window while you are off looking for some lesson plans in another.

- Select preferences to customize how pages appear on your computer.

- Information can be copied from Web pages and pasted into your word processor documents.

- You can get some guidance in Web page creation by selecting "document source" from one of your menus.

Take some time to view other Preferences in the Option menu. You can also customize your browser's mail and newsreader capabilities.

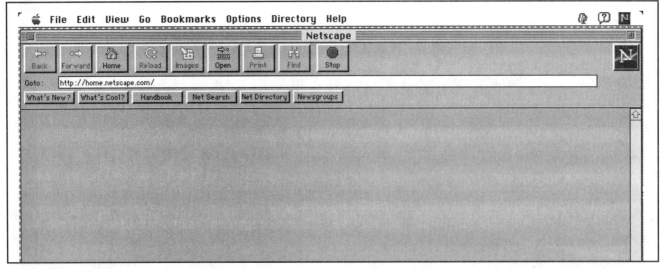

(Netscape Communications, the Netscape Communications logo, Netscape, and Netscape Navigator are trademarks of Netscape Communications Corporation.)

SAMPLE WEB SESSION

I spent just over 23 minutes browsing the World Wide Web for information on whales. As with the other two search chronologies, the italicized words are quotes of what appeared on the screen during the search. Is this the only way to research via the Web? It is not. I am sure you readers will poke holes in my strategy, but it worked for me. I am constantly learning better sites and new tricks. That is half the fun.

1. I went to Yahoo and typed in the keyword "whales."

Results: *I found 15 matches containing whales, displaying matches 1–15.*

2. I followed the link to the Whale Conservation Institute.

http://www.whale.org

I found information on its major programs, such as:

- The Education Programs

- The Right Whale Research Programs

- The Odyssey Ocean Research Program

- The Ecotox Program

3. I followed the link below:

http://curry.edschool.Virginia.EDU./go/Whales/

This page, a class project from Virginia's Curry School of Education, offered a multidisciplinary unit on whales. It is very well done. Its components include teacher resources, lesson plans, student activities, homework suggestions, and links to other whale-related Web sites.

4. I followed the Teacher Resources link from the Whales home page.

5. I followed Lesson Plan link to get an overview of some of their suggested activities. (At the end of this step, I had spent just over six minutes on the Web.)

6. I returned to Yahoo.

7. I followed the link to the Whale Information Network.
   http://www.webmedia.com.au/whales/whales6.html

From this page, I learned that to more accurately identify whales, I should note clues such as

- the shape of the whale's blow hole.

- the presence of other marine mammals.

- the direction and speed of travel.

(Now, the next time I see one, I will be more informed.)

The time elapsed at this point was 11:27.

8. I returned to Yahoo. At the bottom of Yahoo's page, other Web search engines were offered.

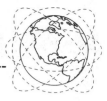

9. I tried Lycos. It already knew I was looking for information on whales. Its results?

I found 2,596 documents matching at least one search term, printing only the first 25 of 150 documents with at least scores of 0.010.

10. I tried Lycos's first hit, "Wildlife Introduction."

The server was either busy or not accepting queries at the time.

11. I wanted to try it again so I made a bookmark for that link.
    http://ics.soe.umich/.edu/projects/web.tracks/map.cgi

12. I followed another Lycos hit called "Whales and Dolphins."
    http://longwood.cs.ucf.edu/~MidLink/whale.html

It was a high-quality whale page created by an 11-year-old student, Shannon Finnegan.

13. I hotlisted/made a bookmark for Lycos' whale search. (It worked beautifully the next time I opened Netscape. I was able to pick up right where I left off and follow many other helpful links.)

My time was up after 23:30 minutes.

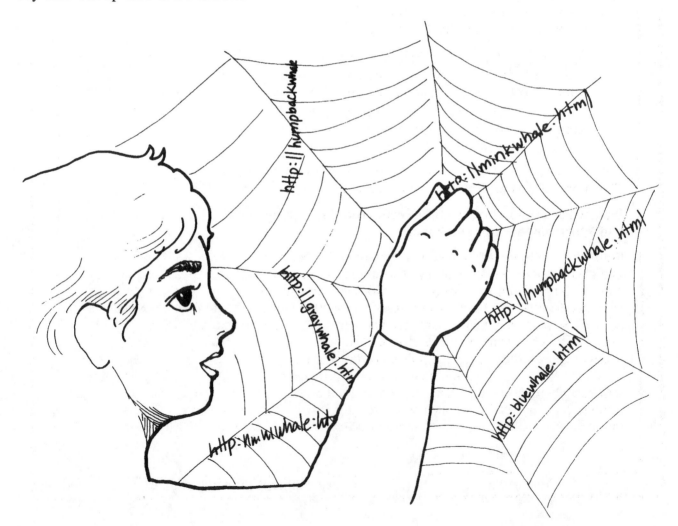

ACCEPTABLE USE POLICIES

Opening Statements

With the widening use of the Internet in schools across the globe, there has been a growing concern about the acceptable use of the Internet in the educational setting. Since there is such a variety of materials accessible through e-mail, on the Internet, and the databases that students access, many educational technology resources are suggesting that school districts develop Acceptable Use Policies. Teachers, students, and parents must read and sign these forms before the students are given access to the Internet at their school. Check with your school administrator to see if your district has developed an AUP. If a policy has not been developed, visit some of the sites below to view some of the many sample AUPs online. Talk to your principal about developing a policy and permission slips for use at your school. Most importantly, make sure that each student who is working online has the following on file:

1. A student-signed form of consent to follow district AUP guidelines

2. A parent-signed form stating awareness of district AUP and releasing the district from responsibility for material that the student may access

3. A student-parent signed form allowing for the release of student work, photographs, or other needed information to be included in collaborative projects, Web pages, or online publication.

Below is a sample of a student-parent permission form from Bellingham Public Schools. The entire AUP is located at the site listed in Some Helpful Internet Sites on page 31.

Parent Permission Letter (an excerpt from the Bellingham Public Schools Internet and Electronic Permission Form)

Students are responsible for good behavior on school computer networks, just as they are in a classroom or school hallway. Communications on the network are often public in nature. General school rules for behavior and communications apply. The network is provided for students to conduct research and communicate with others. Access to network services is given to students who agree to act in a considerate and responsible manner. Parent permission is required. Access is a privilege—not a right. Access entails responsibility. Individual users of the district computer networks are responsible for their behavior and communications over those networks. It is presumed that users will comply with district standards and will honor the agreements they have signed. Beyond the clarification of such standards, the district is not responsible for restricting, monitoring, or controlling the communications of individuals utilizing the network. Users should also not expect that files stored on district servers will always be private.

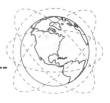

The following will not be permitted by students, teachers, or administrators with district access to the Internet:

- Sending or displaying offensive messages or pictures

- Using obscene language

- Harassing, insulting, or attacking others

- Damaging computers, computer systems, or computer networks

- Violating copyright laws

- Using another's password

- Trespassing in another's folders, work, or files

- Intentionally wasting limited resources

- Employing the network for commercial purposes

Violations may result in a loss of access, as well as other disciplinary or legal action.

User Agreement and Parent Permission Form

As a user of the_____ computer network, I hereby agree to comply with the stated rules—communicating over the network in a reliable fashion while honoring all relevant laws and restrictions.

Student Signature _____

As the parent or legal guardian of the minor student signing above, I grant permission for my son or daughter to access networked computer services such as electronic mail and the Internet. I understand that individuals and families may be held liable for violations. I understand that some materials on the Internet may be objectionable, but I accept responsibility for guidance of Internet use—setting and conveying standards for my daughter or son to follow when selecting, sharing, or exploring information and media.

Parent Signature _____

Date _____

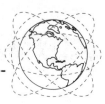

Release to Display Student Work Electronically

Dear Parents/Guardians,

Our class will be collaborating with other classes and publishing our work on the World Wide Web. We could have millions of readers since anyone with access to the Web will be able to view the work we publish. This is an exciting chance to extend our audience, work with partner classes around the globe, and communicate more closely with other "netizens."

By signing the form below, you give your permission for your child's work to be published on the World Wide Web. We are all concerned with the privacy and safety of our students. Because of this, we will honor any and all limitations that you may place on this consent to publish.

Yours truly,

❏ My child's work, in whatever format, may be electronically displayed. His/her first name may be included.

❏ My child's work, in whatever format, may be electronically displayed. Do not include his/her first name.

❏ Photographs of my child may be electronically displayed. His/her first name may be included.

❏ Photographs of my child may be electronically displayed. Do not use his/her first name.

I, _____, give the above teacher and school

permission to produce my child's work electronically. I understand the school and

district Acceptable Use Policies and release the above from any liability resulting from

or connected with publication of my child's work.

_____   _____
            Child   Teacher

_____   _____
   Parent or Guardian Signature   Date

ACCEPTABLE USE POLICIES *(cont.)*

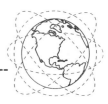

Although having an Acceptable Use Policy in place is helpful, educators and parents alike need to follow a few simple and basic rules regarding Internet access:

1. Supervise the students while they are online.

2. Make sure students are aware of netiquette rules.

3. If access concerns are a big problem, consider creating your own list of sites and providing students with limited access.

4. Monitor communication with other netizens.

5. Use an Internet monitoring program like Surfwatch, Cyberpatrol, or Cybernanny.

6. Review sites your students have visited. Surf through a select number of Web sites to keep yourself up-to-date with places your students are visiting.

Some Helpful Internet Sites

ERIC Gopher menu at: gopher://ericir.syr.edu:70/11/Guides

                              gopher//riceinfo.rice.edu:1170/11/
                              More/Acceptable

Think Quest   http://io.advanced.org/ThinkQuest

Global SchoolNet Foundation   www.gsn.org

TEACHER RESOURCE SITES

The World Wide Web is a treasure trove of teacher resources. Everything from lesson plans to coloring-book pages and grading programs to cooperative projects can be found online. The following sites are just a sampling of the ever growing riches to be mined from the Internet.

Lesson Plans and Project Sites: Why reinvent the wheel when it has already been so well designed and the plans are on the Web? Check out these sites for some great ideas.

Web 66	http://web66.umn.edu/
Global SchoolNet Foundation	http://www.gsn.org
Classroom Connect	www.classroom.net
AskEric (Educational Resource Information Center)	gopher://ericir.syr.edu:70/11/Lesson.
International Classroom Connections	www.stolaf.edu/network/iecc
Projects Home Page	www.eagle.ca/~matink/projects.html
International Society for Technology in Education (ISTE)	http://www.iste.org
Computer Learning Foundation	http://computerlearning.org/
Minnetonka Elementary Science Center	http://www.minnetonka.k12.mn.us/ support/science/index.shtml

Software: Find the Shareware or Freeware that will help you plan lessons, grade programs, create flash cards or change your screensavers. Test-drive some programs before you buy them.

C/net Download.com	http://www.download.com/
The Jumbo Download Network	http://www.jumbo.com/
The Free Zone	http://www.freezone.net/
ZDNet Software Library	http://www.hotfiles.com/

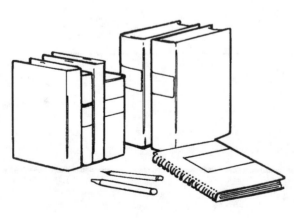 

TEACHER RESOURCE SITES *(cont.)*

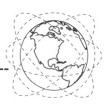

Coloring Pages: Some of these pages can be colored online while others can be printed to color later. Everything's here from ABC and numbers to just plain fun.

Winnie the Pooh and Friends	www.worldkids.net/pooh/
Koris Coloring Book	www.abcs.com/rsanford/color.html
Mark Kistler's 3D Drawing Extravaganza	www.draw3d.com
(from PBS Imagination Station drawing program)	

News Sources: To use a search engine to find a news or media source, point your browser to the search engine of choice; then, in the search dialogue box, enter news. This will give you a hotlist of many. Just a few of the sites are listed below.

CBS News	www.CBS.com
NBC News	www.NBC.com
Electronic Newsstand	www.enews.com

Just for Fun: Looking for information to support a lesson, a site to explore, or just somewhere to play? This is a selection of Web sites that are too much fun to miss.

Bill Nye the Science Guy	http://nyelabs.kcts.org/
The White House	www.whitehouse.gov
NASA	www.NASA.gov
Exploratorium	http://www.exploratorium.org/
The Amazing Fish Cam	www1.netscape.com/fishcam/fishcam.html
Electric Postcard	http://persona.www.media.mit.edu/postcards/
The Electronic Zoo	http://netvet/wustl.edu/e-zoo.htm
Froggy Page	http://frog.simplenet.com/froggy

TASK CARDS

Task cards are mentioned throughout this book. Fill in the information needed for a lesson and then place them next to the computer for easy reference.

site _____

URL _____

site _____

URL _____

site _____

URL _____

site _____

URL _____

CREATING CLASS BOOKMARKS

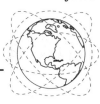

Opening Comments:

Bookmarks, or a hotlist, are a group of Web sites that you may want to revisit often. Add the site to your list, and the next time you want to visit, click on the bookmark button. A pulldown menu will appear from which you can select the name of your site. While it may take time for each student to choose a site to add to the class bookmarks, this is good practice in browsing and presenting new information as well as evaluating quality sites. Be sure to set guidelines for student bookmark choices to keep the subject choices within the educational realm.

Helpful Internet Site(s):

Yahoo	www.yahoo.com
Excite	www.excite.com
Yahooligans	www.yahooligans.com (a great child-oriented search engine)
Lycos	www.lycos.com
Webcrawler	www.webcrawler.com

Setting the Stage:

- Practice making bookmarks (see page 23 for Netscape's toolbar).
  —When you find a site you will want to revisit later, click on the "bookmark" button.
  —Choose the "Add to Bookmark" option.

- Copy the bookmark instructions on page 36 to place by the computer for student reference.

- Model how to create a bookmark. (Explain that most browsers allow you to edit the name of the selected site for clearer titles.)

- Make a task card with the steps to follow. Put this by the computer for reference.

- Discuss the criteria and deadline for acceptance of a Web site into the class list.

- Discuss student expectations: (1) Add a Web site to the class bookmarks. (2) Be so familiar with the site that you can present it to a group of students or the whole class.

Criteria for Acceptance of a Web Site into the Class Hall of Fame

1. Site fits into the assigned theme (if there is one).

2. Site is fun.

3. Site is educational.

4. Student can clearly state why the Web site is of educational value.

Procedure:

- Students need to review the criteria and look for new/interesting sites.

- Students will complete the worksheet on page 37.

- Students should review the site before making any presentations.

- Students will present their sites to the class (or a chosen group).

CREATING CLASS BOOKMARKS *(cont.)*

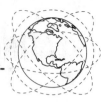

Special Considerations:

- You could have students choose new bookmarks when a new theme or subject is covered in class. Divide bookmarks alphabetically by theme, by group project, etc.

- Have students share their bookmark information on any mailing lists you participate in.

- Students could publish the best bookmarks, categorized by subject, in school flyers or papers.

- For good public relations and further collaboration, have students inform the chosen site's Web master that the site has qualified for the class bookmarks. (Be sure to include the criteria for selection.)

Make a Bookmark

1. Browse through some Internet sites.

2. When you find a site you want, click the **bookmark** button.

3. Click **add to bookmarks**.

Explore the Net

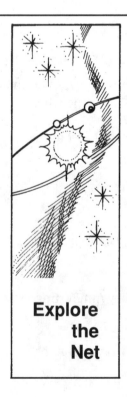

Explore the Net

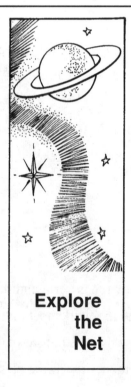

Explore the Net

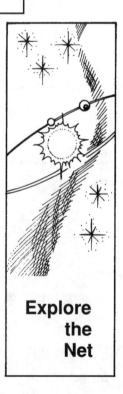

Explore the Net

CREATING CLASS BOOKMARKS *(cont.)*

Site Name: _____

URL: _____

This site is   **GREAT**   **GOOD**   **OK**

because of the following:

_____

_____

_____

The best part of this site is the following:

_____

_____

_____

_____

What I learned from this Web site:

_____

_____

_____

_____

CURRENT EVENTS

Opening Comments:

Informing our students about the world around them is our job as educators. Many teachers have a current events time line to help students make sense of news reports. Now send students online to gather this information from a variety of sources.

Some Helpful Internet Sites:

Yahooligans Newspaper hotlist — http://www.yahooligans.com/The_Scoop/Newspapers/

Yahoo (Choose "News") — http://www.yahoo.com

Yahoo: News and Media:Newspapers:K–12 (student-created newspapers) — http://www.yahoo.com/News_and_Media /Newspapers/K_12/

Setting the Stage:

- Make bookmarks of sites to visit or put the URLs on cards at the computer.
- Copy "My Current Event," page 39.
- Define current events for your class. Decide on, discuss, and post any limitations on the type of news that you may want to bring into the classroom.
- Role-play and practice current event reports with your students.

Procedure:

- Students visit Web sites to gather news stories.
- Students print information from the Web site and then summarize it on their worksheets.

Special Considerations and Other Options:

- When studying another culture or country, have students look for news articles about that culture. For example, if your class is studying Mexico, the news articles could be about relations with Mexico, or they could be news from Mexico.
- Follow a topic that interests the students for a week or so. Keep copies of the articles posted so students can revisit them.
- Have students look for news articles relating to a science or math theme.
- Post a world map. Put a push pin in at each spot from which a current event is reported.
- Perhaps have one or two students be "reporters" for a week. They spend a few days the previous week looking for news articles and summarizing them on their current event page. These reporters will then spend the next week giving oral current event reports to the class.

CURRENT EVENTS *(cont.)*

My Current Event

Who:_____

Where:_____

What Happened:

    1. _____

    2. _____

    3. _____

My Current Event

Who:_____

Where:_____

What Happened:

    1. _____

    2. _____

    3. _____

VIRTUAL FIELD TRIPS

Opening Comments:

Would you like to take your students on more field trips, but (a) there are limited drivers for trips, and/or (b) the places you want to visit are too far away? Don't limit yourself or the curriculum. Review your lesson plans and take your class on a virtual field trip instead.

Some Helpful Internet Sites:

Mark Twain's Birthplace and Hometown	http://www.lijnet.or.jp/robagoya/mt/mtpage.htm
Virtual Tour—McMurdo Station, Antarctica	http://astro.uchicago.edu/cara/vtour/mcmurdo
Virtual Williamsburg	http://www.gc.net/wol/wol.html
White House	http://www.whitehouse.gov
Crayola Crayon	http://www.crayola.com/crayola/
Hands-on Children's Museum	http://www.wln.com/~deltapac/hocm.html
Children's Museum of Indianapolis	http://www.a1.com/children/exhibit.htm
Lego	http://www.lego.com/
Grand Canyon	http://www.kaibab.org/grand.htm

*Use a search engine to help you find other places like museums and national parks.

Setting the Stage:

- Choose the place you want students to visit. Find a tour that fits into a theme you are studying or a place that is of special interest to your students.
- Make bookmarks of sites to visit or put the URLs on cards at the computer.
- Complete a KWL chart with your class. This preview can provide a good springboard for student questions.
- Copy and review the Field Trip Logs with students.

Procedure:

- The teacher or students decide on two questions to answer from the field trip visit and write these on their Field Trip Logs.
- Students work alone or in pairs to view a field trip site.
- Children fill in the answers to complete their Field Trip Logs.

Special Considerations and Other Options:

- Post completed papers on a bulletin board of work related to the field trip topic. For instance, if the White House is being studied, post Field Trip Logs that answer student questions about the White House.
- If printers are available, have students print information from the Web sites they visited.
- Print-screens of Web site pictures can be a great addition to a class book about the unit of study or to illustrate information gathered by the students.
- For younger students, or those who have difficulty reading and writing, assign a scavenger hunt of sorts. In this case, students need to find certain pictures, sounds, or images at the site.

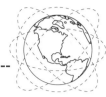

VIRTUAL FIELD TRIPS *(cont.)*

Field Trip Log

1. Write down two questions about this field trip site.
2. Go to the site and look for the answers to your questions. Write the answers below.

SITE:_____

URL:_____

Question #1: _____

_____

_____

Answer #1:_____

_____

Question #2: _____

_____

Answer #2:_____

_____

_____

GOING BUGGY!

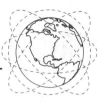

Opening Comments:

Most children love to find out about the bugs and insects in their world. Use the lessons on the following pages in a number of different ways to share information about this intriguing part of our lives. Students find information online and then move offline to finish their worksheets. These pages could be completed as homework, cooperative lessons, in stations, or as a whole class.

Some Helpful Internet Sites:

Monarch Watch	www.MonarchWatch.org
Butterfly World Experience	www.introweb.com/butterfly/welcome.htm
Minnetonka Elementary Science Center	www.minnetonka.k12.mn.us/support/science/index.html
Virtual Arthropod Zoo	www.azstarnet.com/~sasi/arthzoo/clasindx.htm
Minibeast World	www.tesser.com/minibeast/3lesson.htm
Entomology (Biosciences)	www.colostate.edu/Depts/Entomology/images.html
Children's Butterfly Site	www.mesc.ribs.gov/Butterfly.html

Setting the Stage:

- Complete the Insect Know, Want to Know, Learned (KWL) chart as a class.
- Make bookmarks of sites to visit or put the URLs on cards at the computer.
- Discuss the differences between bugs and insects and review basic insect anatomy.
- Put up word charts/posters to review the vocabulary.
- Have insect reference books and picture books available for student work time.
- Perhaps, download pictures from Children's Butterfly Site.

Procedure:

- Review the worksheets and directions with the students.
- Give students time to browse the sites.
- While online, students look for insects, pictures of the metamorphic stages, and information to add to the KWL chart completed as a class.
- For the metamorphosis page, have students draw the different stages of metamorphosis.
- On the collection sheet, have students find a set amount of insects before filling in the information.
- Students complete their collection sheets and Metamorphosis worksheets.

Special Considerations and Other Options:

- Participate in the Amazing Insects data collection project at the Minnetonka Web site. Trudy Schnorr and Barbara Kostial have authored this continuing online project.
- As an option, have students draw and label insects and bugs to use as posters in the room.
- Students could use other materials for the metamorphosis worksheet. When glued onto this page, poppy seeds, macaroni, and cottonballs work well as eggs, larva, and cocoon.

GOING BUGGY! *(cont.)*

Insects and Bugs Collection Sheet

Kind	Description (What does it look like?)	Insect or Bug	Comments

GOING BUGGY! *(cont.)*

Insects and Bugs K-W-L Chart

What do you know?	What do you want to know?	What did you learn?

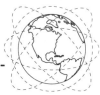

GOING BUGGY! *(cont.)*

Insects and Bugs Metamorphosis

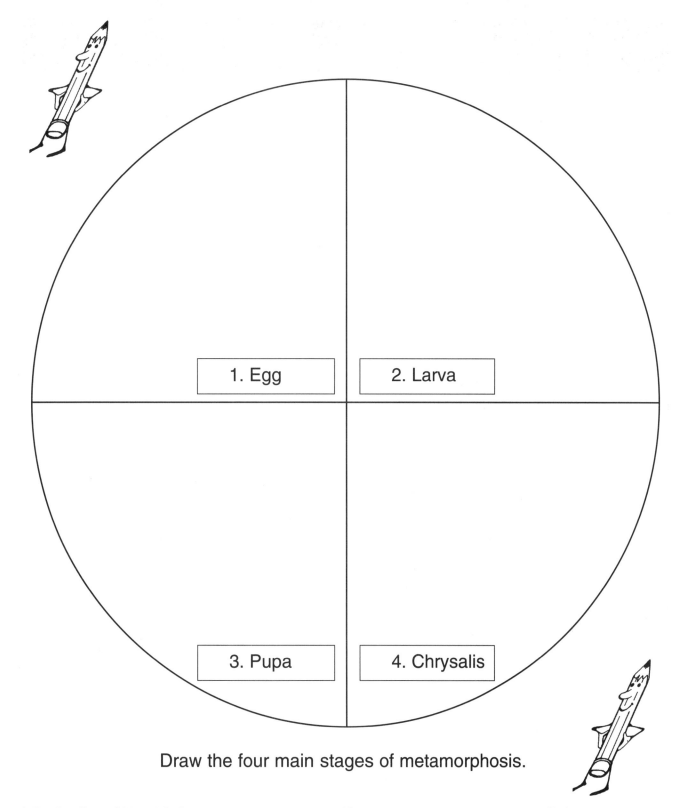

Draw the four main stages of metamorphosis.

#2187 Internet for Kids

THE WORLD OF WINNIE THE POOH

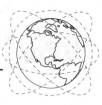

Opening Comments:

Not many children can resist the stories of Winnie the Pooh and his friends in the *Hundred Acre Wood*. Use that interest to inspire your curriculum. The sites below have many activities, games, coloring pages, and stories to share with your students. Send your students on a scavenger hunt to find some of these jewels.

Some Helpful Internet Sites:

In Which Pooh Has Many Adventures and We Get to Join Him	http://qru.com/gallery/pooh/index.html
The Page at Pooh Corner	www.public.iastate.edu/~jmilne/pooh.html
Pooh's Corner	http:voyager.cns.ohiou.edu/~bkeys/
Eeyore's Thistly Hideaway	www.depeche.mode.net/~milliner/ michelle/eeyore1.html
World of Winnie the Pooh	www.dlcwest.com/~obusti11

Setting the Stage:

* Visit the sites before letting your students loose. If you are looking for stories written by A.A. Milne, be aware that while Web masters try to be careful, stories that were once located on a page may later be removed due to copyright laws.
* Make bookmarks of the chosen sites, or put the URLs on task cards near the computer.
* Describe a scavenger hunt and its rules to your students.
* Review the scavenger hunt pages with the class.

Procedure:

* Students visit the Web sites and look for the items requested on the "Hunting for Pooh" pages.

Special Considerations and Other Options:

* Have students work with partners to complete their hunt.
* If some page names are difficult to find, ask students to write the URL or the page name.
* As students get more proficient, have them download pictures of their characters and note the site location.
* Have students write down the rules to play a game of Pooh Sticks. Play a tournament.
* If you find stories online, have students read one and then illustrate it themselves.
* After students have been reading stories online, make a class book of student illustrations.

THE WORLD OF WINNIE THE POOH *(cont.)*

A Few Answers for the Scavenger Hunt (There are many possibilities.)

1. Virtual Pooh Sticks — http://pooh.muscat.co.uk/pooh-sticks/
   Winnie the Pooh Expotition [sic] — www.worldkids.net/pooh

2. Sunset's Index of ftp/pub/pictures/fantasy/Pooh — http://ftp.sunset.se/ftp/pub/pictures/fantasy/Pooh/100acregif

3. Eeyore's Thistly Hideaway — www.depeche.mode.net/~milliner/michelle/eeyore1.html
   Galleon's Lap — www.teleport.com/%7Erbpenn/pooh.html

4. Winnie The Pooh Expotition — www.worldkids.net/pooh
   Eeyore's Thistly Hideaway — www.depeche.mode.net/~milliner/michelle/eeyore1.html
   Pooh's Corner — http://voyager.cns.ohiou.edu/~bkeys/

5. The World of Winnie the Pooh — www.dlcwest.com/~obustill
   Pooh's Corner — http://voyager.cns.ohiou.edu/~bkeys/

6. Page at Pooh Corner — www.public.iastate.edu/~jmilne/pooh.html
   Welcome to Pooh Corner — www.pooh-corner.com

7. Pooh's Corner — http://voyager.cns.ohiou.edu/~bkeys
   Galleon's Lap — www.teleport.com/%7Erbpenn/pooh.html

8. Eeyore's Thistly Hideaway — www.depeche.mode.net/~milliner/michelle/eeyore1.html
   Winnie the Pooh Expotition [sic] — www.worldkids.net/pooh

THE WORLD OF WINNIE THE POOH *(cont.)*

Hunting for Pooh

1. Which character will you look for?

   ❏   Winnie the Pooh   ❏ Owl   ❏ Rabbit

   ❏   Piglet   ❏ Kanga   ❏ Roo

   ❏   Christopher Robin   ❏ Tigger   ❏ Eeyore

2. Find the rules to play Pooh Sticks.

   Site: _____

   URL: _____

3. Find a picture of your character.

   Site: _____

   URL: _____

4. Where's a map of the *100-Acre Wood*?

   Site: _____

   URL: _____

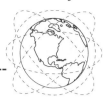

THE WORLD OF WINNIE THE POOH *(cont.)*

Hunting for Pooh *(cont.)*

5. List a site that plays music.

   Site: _____

   URL: _____

6. This site has a biography of A. A. Milne.

   Site: _____

   URL: _____

7. There is a Winnie the Pooh story at this site.

   Site: _____

   URL: _____

8. Find a site that has Pooh coloring pages.

   Site: _____

   URL: _____

ORIGAMI ORIGINALS

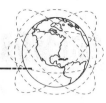

Opening Comments:

The ability to create a box, plane, hat, or even a kangaroo from paper has fascinated children of all ages for many years. The ancient art of Japanese paper folding, origami, is a enjoyable, habit-forming method of teaching the geometry of basic shapes and angles to elementary school students.

Some Helpful Internet Sites:

Jasper's Origami Menagerie	www.cytex.com/go/jasper/origami
Alex Bateman's Origami Page	www.mrc-cpe.cam.ac.uk/jong/agb/origami.html
School Art	http:jw.stanford.edu/KIDS/SCHOOL/ART/kids_arts.html
Nick Robinsonn's Origami Site	www.cheesypeas.demon.co.uk/diagrams.html
Alex Barber's Origami Page	www.the-village.com/origami/index.html

Setting the Stage:

- Make bookmarks of sites to visit that have models or put the URLs on cards at the computer.
- Cut lightweight paper into 6" (15 cm) squares or purchase origami folding paper.
- Practice basic folds with the class.
- Begin with the simple model level as some origami folding can get quite difficult.
- Perhaps train a couple of students as origami masters so they can troubleshoot any folding difficulties the class may have.

Procedure:

Step 1: Folding

- Students visit some Web sites and decide on a shape to create.
- Using the models at their site, students fold an origami creation.
- Students may print the models or fold their creations while online.

Step 2: Browsing Through the Galleries

- Several of the sites mentioned above have "galleries" of photographs showing origami creations.
- Before or after making their creations, students browse through the Origami sites and list something found there. This information can then be recorded on the "Origami Originals Worksheet" on page 51.

Special Considerations and Other Options:

- You may want to make a poster that demonstrates and labels a few of the basic folds.
- Another possibility is to have students visit an assigned site to create a certain model.
- Use this page to tie into a unit on Japan, geometric shapes, or animals.

ORIGAMI ORIGINALS *(cont.)*

Origami Originals Worksheet

Site:_____

URL: _____

I found something at this site that I want to share with you. I found _____

_____

_____

_____

_____

- -

Site:_____

URL: _____

I found something at this site that I want to share with you. I found _____

_____

_____

_____

_____

RAIN FOREST STATIONS

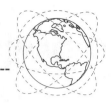

Opening Comments:

Stations can be an enjoyable, hands-on method of passing along information. The activities on the following pages are a follow-up after students have discussed the rain forest and visited several Web sites. Students have booklets to complete as they move around the room. These booklets can be sent home or saved for display at Open House.

Some Helpful Internet Sites

Rain Forest Action Network	www.ran.org
Kids Action (RAN)	www.ran.org/ran/Kids_action/index.html
Rain Forest Alliance	www.rainforest-alliance.org/ktm.html
Indonesia Rain Forest Tour	www.geocities.com/RainForest/3678/home.html
Surinam Rain Forest Page	www.euronet.nl/users/mbleeker/suri_eng.html

The Activities

What's That Smell?

In this activity, students smell an item and then try to identify what it is. They then choose the picture that matches their guess and glue it into their station booklet.

Preparation:

1. Visit some of the suggested Internet sites to find a list of rain forest products that are available to you. (suggestions: cinnamon, vanilla, nutmeg, pineapple, banana, coffee beans, coconut, grapefruit, cloves, chili pepper, chocolate, ginger)
2. Collect some small, closed containers (film canisters work very well). Label them A–F.
3. Place an item to be identified in each container.
4. Copy the instruction pages and put them on cards at each station.
5. Copy the pictures (if you decide to use them) for students to put in their booklets.

Mystery Items

In this activity, students reach into an enclosed container (a sock in a cup), try to identify the item inside, and then choose the picture that matches their guess and glue it into their station booklet.

Preparation:

1. Copy the instruction pages and put them on cards at each station.
2. Visit some of the suggested Internet sites to find a list of rain forest products that are available to you. (suggestions: sesame seeds, peanuts, avocado, pineapple, banana, balsa wood, gum (chicle), rubber, jute (rope, twine), coffee beans, coconut, vanilla bean)
3. Place small plastic cups into several socks. These will be the "guessing containers." Label them A–F.
4. Place an item to be identified in each of the cups.
5. Copy the pictures (if you decide to use them) for students to put in their booklets.

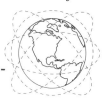

RAIN FOREST STATIONS *(cont.)*

Who Lives in the Rain Forest?

At this station, students draw their own idea of what the rain forest looks like.

Preparation:

1. Cut blank paper to match the size of the booklet.
2. Have many colors available to students for the drawing. If possible, use a variety of media as well. Let students use chalk, paint, pastels, markers, crayons. . . whatever you have on hand.
3. Have pictures and books about the rain forest at the station for students to look through.

Tour a Rain Forest

This station is best run by an adult or older student who can guide the group on a virtual tour of a rain forest. Students will take a tour and list forest inhabitants in their booklets.

Preparation:

1. Long before deciding to use this station, visit some of the suggested Internet sites and find a park to tour.
2. Copy the instruction page and put it on a card at the station.
3. Set up the class computer with the browser pointed at the site chosen in step one.
4. In the small group, students click through the rain forest.
5. As they tour, students put the names of plants, animals, insects, and other rain forest inhabitants into their booklets.

Create an Insect

After reminding students of an insect's basic anatomy (three body parts and six legs), let your class loose to create their own species of insect. Add these creations to a class rain forest.

Preparation:

1. Copy the instruction page and put it on a card at the station.
2. Copy the "Insect Body Shapes" for each student or
3. make patterns of the body shapes on oaktag so the students can trace the shapes they want.
4. Have construction paper, glue, and scissors available.

RAIN FOREST STATIONS *(cont.)*

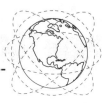

What's That Smell?

1. Visit some Web sites. Find some items that you could smell at school.

   Rain Forest Action Network www.ran.org

   Kids Action (RAN)   www.ran.org/ran/Kids_action/index.html

   Rain Forest Alliance   www.rainforest-alliance.org/ktm.html

2. Smell the contents of each container.

3. Find the picture that matches the smell and put it in your book under the correct letter.

Mystery Items?

1. Visit some Web sites. Find some items that you might be able to touch at school.

   Rain Forest Action Network www.ran.org

   Kids Action (RAN)   www.ran.org/ran/Kids_action/index.html

   Rain Forest Alliance   www.rainforest-alliance.org/ktm.html

2. Place your hand in the cups.

3. Without looking, try to guess what is in them.

4. Place the picture that shows the item under the matching letter.

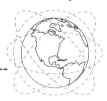

RAIN FOREST STATIONS *(cont.)*

What's That Smell?

Smell the contents of each container. Place the picture that shows the smell under the matching letter.

A	B	C	D	E	F

What's That Smell?

Smell the contents of each container. Place the picture that shows the smell under the matching letter.

A	B	C	D	E	F

RAIN FOREST STATIONS *(cont.)*

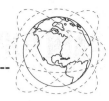

Mystery Items?

Place your hand in the cups. Without looking, try to guess what is in them.
Place the picture that shows the item under the matching letter.

A	B	C	D	E	F

Mystery Items?

Place your hand in the cups. Without looking, try to guess what is in them.
Place the picture that shows the item under the matching letter.

A	B	C	D	E	F

56

RAIN FOREST STATIONS *(cont.)*

What's That Smell?

cinnamon	lemon	vanilla	pineapple
cloves	nutmeg	ginger	black pepper
chocolate	coconut	tea	coffee

Mystery Items?

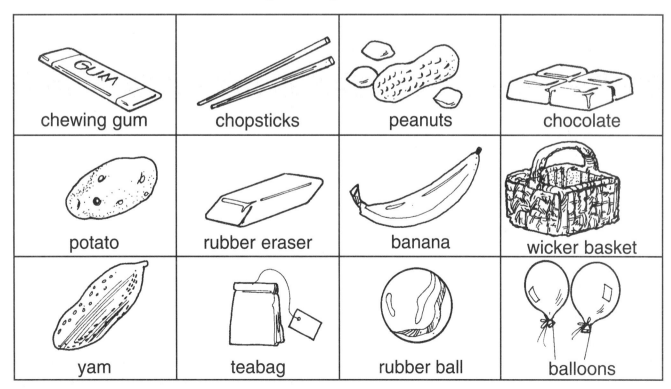

chewing gum	chopsticks	peanuts	chocolate
potato	rubber eraser	banana	wicker basket
yam	teabag	rubber ball	balloons

RAIN FOREST STATIONS *(cont.)*

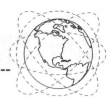

Create an Insect

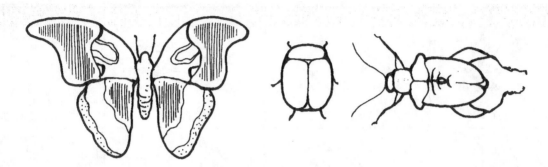

1. Visit a Web site to view insects. Notice the special shapes that make insects.

    Rain Forest Action Network www.ran.org

    Kids Action (RAN)   www.ran.org/ran/Kids_action/index.html

    Rain Forest Alliance   www.rainforest-alliance.org/ktm.html

2. Pick the shapes you want to make your insect.
3. Trace and cut the shapes out of colored paper.
4. Glue the insect together and give it a name.

Tour a Rain forest

1. Use the Internet to take a tour of a rain forest.

    Indonesia Rain Forest Tour www.geocities.com
                                 /RainForest/3678/home.html

    Surinam Rain Forest Page www.euronet.nl/users/mbleeker/suri_eng.html

    Amazon Adventure   http://vif27.icair.iac.org.nz

2. As you move through the Web site, put the names of the animals, insects, plants, and other creatures that you see into your booklet.

RAIN FOREST STATIONS *(cont.)*

Tour a Rain Forest

Animals	Plants	Insects	Others

Animals	Plants	Insects	Others
ocelot	kapok tree	toucan	macadamia nuts
jaguar	emerald tree boa	harpy eagle	mango
elephant	poison arrow frog	morpho butterfly	banana
bromeliad	three-toed sloth	cacao	rubber tree

Tour a Rain Forest

Animals	Plants	Insects	Others

Animals	Plants	Insects	Others
ocelot	kapok tree	toucan	macadamia nuts
jaguar	emerald tree boa	harpy eagle	mango
elephant	poison arrow frog	morpho butterfly	banana
bromeliad	three-toed sloth	cacao	rubber tree

GO WILD WITH SHEL SILVERSTEIN

Opening Comments:

Are your students familiar with the "Meehoo"? What about the "Picture Puzzle Piece" or "Hector the Collector"? Help your students explore the world of poetry through the words of Shel Silverstein.

Some Helpful Internet Sites:

Quix's Shel Silverstein Page   http://www.dmv.com/~quix/shel.html

Shel Silverstein   http://area51.upsu.plym.ac.uk/~pookie/literary.shel.html

A little poetry anyone?   http://www.cen.uiuc.edu/~jsporter/dots_corner.html

Setting the Stage:

* Decide which chart your students will be using and review the directions with them.
* Review rhyming words and word families with the class (hat, cat, bat, sat).
* Help students generate a list of rhyming words to post in the room for reference.
* Make bookmarks of sites to visit or put the URLs on cards at the computer.

Procedure:

* Students visit a Web site and read a work by Shel Silverstein.
* Students use their Silverstein Rhymes charts to list the rhyming words found at the site.
* For the "Rhymes With" page, students read from a Web site.
* They copy a line from the poem and then write their own line that rhymes with the original Silverstein line.

Special Considerations and Other Options:

* Students may want to work in groups to write a rhyming sequel to a work by Mr. Silverstein.
* Have students illustrate some of the poetry. Then show them the original illustrations.
* Students could choose their favorite poem and draw a picture based on one line.
* Assign a poem to a group of students. Have each pick a line to copy and illustrate.
* Use this activity as a springboard to student poetry writing.
* Have students print a poem from one of the suggested Web sites. Students then write their own poem, inspired by the one they printed. Place these pages next to each other in a classroom poetry book. Be sure to include credits to the authors and Web sites.

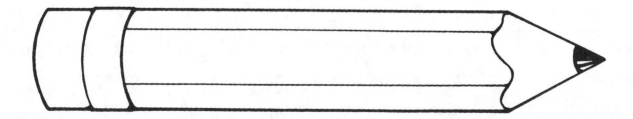

GO WILD WITH SHEL SILVERSTEIN *(cont.)*

Silverstein Rhymes

Directions: Read a Shel Silverstein poem on the Internet. On the form below, write the words you find that rhyme.

Web Site: _____

URL: _____

Word	Rhymes With

GO WILD WITH SHEL SILVERSTEIN *(cont.)*

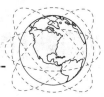

Rhymes With . . .

Directions: Go to a Shel Silverstein Web site and read a poem. Copy a sentence from a poem to your paper. Write a second sentence that rhymes with the one you found at the Web site.

Web Site: _____

URL:_____

Silverstein line:_____

_____

My line:_____

_____

Silverstein line:_____

_____

My line:_____

_____

STORYBOOKS

Opening Comments:

Superheroes, cartoon characters, and storybook heroes are an important part of the young child's world. Bring your students' interests into the classroom. Help them create stories that involve their favorite characters.

Some Helpful Internet Sites:

Cartoon World   www.cet.com/~rascal/welcome.html

Looney Tunes   www.personal.usyd.edu.au/~swishart/looney.html

World of Winnie the Pooh   www.machaon.tu/pooh/index.html

Disney   www.dlcwest.com/~obustill

Setting the Stage:

- Choose and copy the storybook pages that are best for your students. The fill-in-the-blank forms on the following pages are designed for different ability levels. Use the one(s) that fit your grade level or make new ones.
- Make bookmarks of sites to visit or put the URLs on cards at the computer.
- Review the story sheets and directions with the students.
- Make an overhead or poster of the Words to Use chart on page 69. Complete this chart with the class before they go online. Keep it posted for student reference during story writing.

Procedure:

Preposition Book: In this storybook, students insert the name of their character on the blank to show the prepositions to, under, over, beside, in, and on.

- Copy the preposition storybook as is, or cut it apart so each sentence is on a separate page.
- Give students time to read about or choose their characters at the sites.
- Students complete their story sheets alone, in partners or in groups.
- Have students illustrate each sentence of their story.

Once Upon a Time: This format is a bit more difficult. Students have more blanks to fill in and more word choices to make.

- Students read about or choose their characters on the Web.
- Students complete their storybooks.
- Have authors make cover illustrations for their storybooks.

Special Considerations and Other Options:

- Some sites, like the Looney Tunes® site, are just graphics. These can still be a good source for pictures and writing ideas.
- Group stories by main character or by setting before binding.
- Collect each student's stories throughout the year and bind them all together as a book for that child.

STORYBOOKS *(cont.)*

A Story Form for Prepositions

_____ went **to** the _____.

                       character's name

He crawled **under** the _____.

He flew **over** the _____.

_____ sat **beside** the _____.

                       character's name

She ate **in** the _____.

Finally, _____ sat **on** the _____.

                character's name

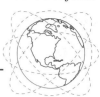

STORYBOOKS *(cont.)*

A Story Form for Once Upon a Time

_____
title

Once upon a time in an old _____, there lived
place (setting)

_____. He was a very special _____ who
main character   noun

loved to _____.
verb

One day, _____ heard a shout from the
main character

_____. "Help! I'm stuck in the
noun (a place)

_____." So _____ rushed to the
noun   main character

_____. He was shocked to see _____, his
same place   name

best friend.

"How did you get there?" asked _____.
main character

"Well, I was walking down the _____ when a
noun

_____ appeared. I said _____ and
villain   greeting

the _____ cast a _____. Help me
villain   noun

get out of this mess!"

STORYBOOKS *(cont.)*

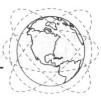

A Story Form for Once Upon a Time *(cont.)*

"You _____ here while I _____ that
   verb   verb

_____."
        villain

That evening, _____ finally found the
                main character

_____. All day, _____ wondered how to get the
    villain   main character

_____ to remove the _____. By the
    villain   noun

early evening, he had a plan. As the _____ came down the
                                          villain

road, our hero held out a magic _____. Now, we all know
                                       noun

that _____ cannot resist a magic _____.
          villain   noun

Sure enough, the _____ stopped and tried to take the magic
                    villain

_____ from _____'s hand.
       noun   main character

   "Not so fast!" said _____. "First of all, you must
                          main character

remove the _____ from my friend,
                  noun

_____."
     name

   "Why should I?" snarled the _____.
                                   villain

STORYBOOKS *(cont.)*

A Story Form for Once Upon a Time *(cont.)*

"Because _____ is a good _____,
name   noun

and _____ is my friend," answered
personal pronoun

_____.
main character

"Will you promise to give me another magic _____
noun

when I do as you ask?" said the _____.
villain

"Certainly," said _____.
main character

So the two returned to _____ where,
noun (place)

_____ was still waiting to be rescued and have the
name

_____ removed.
noun

"_____," said the _____. As
magic words   villain

quick as a wink, _____ was free. Our hero,
name

_____, kept his promise and gave the _____
main character   villain

another magic _____ before warning that if
noun

_____
personal pronoun

STORYBOOKS *(cont.)*

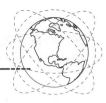

A Story Form for Once Upon a Time *(cont.)*

wanted to return to that area, the _____ would have to be nice
villain

to the people. The _____ agreed to follow the rules and said
villain

goodbye to _____ and his
main character

friend_____.
name

This is a picture of my favorite part of the story.

STORYBOOKS *(cont.)*

Words to Use

Nouns	Verbs

LOVE THAT LAVA

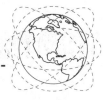

Opening Comments:

Combine earth science, geography, and geology in this exploration of the world's volcanoes. There are two lessons in this section. The first has students asking questions of volcanologists. In the second, students map the locations of major volcanos. It may be difficult to move on once your students find all the stimulating activities waiting for them at Volcano World. Just go with the flow.

Some Helpful Internet Sites:

Volcano World   http://volcano.und.nodak.edu

Global Volcanism Program: Volcano NetLinks   http://www.volcano.si.edu/gvp/links/index.htm

Setting the Stage:

Ask a Volcanologist:

- Make bookmarks of sites to visit or put the URLs on cards at the computer.
- Complete a KWL chart with the class. Assign or have students decide on the questions to be asked before going online. Students write their question on the "Ask a Volcanologist" page.
- Define terms. Possibly put up a poster with definitions.
- You may want to have children make a volcano logbook with a glossary and space to take notes of information found online.

World Volcano Map:

- Make bookmarks of sites to visit or put the URLs on cards at the computer.
- Copy the world map on page 72.
- Review the map and instructions with students.

Procedure:

Ask a Volcanologist:

- Children visit one of the Web sites above and find the section about asking questions.
- Students determine if their question has already been answered. If so, write down the response to share with the class.
- If the question has not been answered by an expert at the site, then e-mail the question. When an answer is posted, share the response with the class.

World Volcano Map:

- Students browse through volcano sites to find the geographic locations of volcanoes around the world.
- Students mark their world maps to show locations. Volcano names are written in spaces below the map.
- Another option is to have students label their volcano maps with the longitude and latitude of the volcano locations. (This information is available at the Volcano World site).

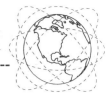

LOVE THAT LAVA *(cont.)*

Special Considerations and Other Options:

- Students could go to Volcano World and read the stories about *Rocky the Volcano Creature* by Jean Kurtz.

- Have children illustrate a scene from one of Ms. Kurtz's stories. Make a classroom display of the text along with student illustrations. Another option is to have students send their pictures to the Web master for inclusion in the story.

- Take your students on a current-event tour of volcanic activity in Volcano World's volcanic activity database. This source is frequently updated and includes satellite images of current eruptions.

Ask a Volcanologist

1. Write your volcano question on the lines below.
2. Go to a volcano Web site and find the section about asking questions.
3. Look for your question.
4. If it has already been answered, write the answer on the lines below.
5. If your question has not been answered, send your question to the experts. Once you get an answer, write it on your form and share the information with the class.

My Question: _____

_____

_____

_____

The Expert's Answer: _____

_____

_____

_____

LOVE THAT LAVA *(cont.)*

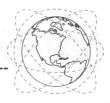

1. Go to a Web site and find the location of several volcanoes.
2. On the map, write a different number for each volcano you find.
3. Write the volcano names in the lines below the map. Make sure each volcano name matches the number you wrote on the map.

1._____ 2._____

3._____ 4._____

5._____ 6._____

7._____ 8._____

WEATHER LOGS

Opening Comments:

Many of us have our students make daily weather reports as part of the classroom opening. Add onto that practice by collecting data from a weather service and recording the information in personal log books.

Some Helpful Internet Sites:

Rice University—The Climate/Weather/Earth Hotlist   http://space.rice.edu/~rss/hotlist.html

Country Weather Center   http://ny.frontiercomm.net/
~airplane/weather.htm

USA Today Weather   www.usatoday.com/weather/wfront.htm

Weather World 2010 Project   ww2010.atmos.uiuc.edu/(GH)
/home.ixml

Setting the Stage:

- Discuss weather and cloud formations with your students.
- Introduce the thermometer, degrees Celsius, and degrees Fahrenheit.
- Practice reading a thermometer.
- Discuss what forecasters mean by the high and low temperature.
- Make bookmarks of sites to visit, or put the URLs on cards at the computer.
- Bind pages into books for each student to use. Leave the cover blank.

Procedure:

- Students decorate the covers of their weather logs.
- Visit sites each day for a week or for the duration of the weather unit.
- Students complete the booklet pages to show weather activity in their local area.

Special Considerations and Other Options:

- Have students watch the evening weather report to compare the Internet forecast to what actually happened in the area's weather.
- Explore the *USA Today* site for further activities to use with your students. They have a wonderful section on cloud formations and what causes them and or cloud images.
- Use this lesson in conjunction with an extended unit on weather. Keep the completed log books for display in a showcase portfolio or for Open House.
- Another possibility is to have students track severe weather activity in another part of the world.
- If you are studying other countries, such as Japan, have a group of students keep a log on the weather patterns in Japan for the week.
- Further discuss how the weather patterns affect the biome in a certain area. For instance, what effect does weather have on rain forests?

WEATHER LOGS *(cont.)*

Weather Log

Today's weather forecast is _____

_____

_____

_____

The high temperature today will be _____ degrees

Fahrenheit_____ degrees Celsius.

The low temperature will be _____ degrees

Fahrenheit_____ degrees Celsius.

The weather outside looks

sunny	cloudy	rainy	snowy

WHAT'S COOKING?

Opening Comments:

Children love to cook. What better way can there be to introduce students to fractions, measurement, chemical reactions, direction following, and the many other concepts cooking entails? Send your class today to explore the kitchens on the World Wide Web.

Some Helpful Internet Sites:

Thanksgiving (history and tips)	www.2020tech.com/thanks
Kellogg's Rice Krispies Recipes Galore	www.treatsrecipes.com/home.asp
Kids Cooking Club	www.kidscook.com
Ragu Homepage	www.eat.com
Kosher Express	www.marketnet.com/mktnet/kosher/recipes/index.html
Campbell's Community	www.campbellsoup.com

Setting the Stage:

- Make bookmarks of sites to visit or put the URLs on cards at the computer.
- Have students find out the nation(s) of their family ancestry and choose a recipe from that nation. For instance, since my family's roots are in so many countries, my sons usually choose Germany as a place to study.
- Make a copy of the "Recipe Card" form for each student.
- Review the instructions with the class.

Procedure:

- Students are assigned (or decide on) a recipe type to retrieve.
- Students visit a site and choose a recipe.
- Students write their recipes on the "Recipe Card" form or print it out.

Special Considerations and Other Options:

- Divide students into teams. Have them research recipes by topic: holiday, pasta, Italian recipes, party food, desserts, whatever topic you wish.
- Have a class feast. Students prepare and bring in dishes they discovered online.
- Cook some of the recipes in class.
- Tie this lesson into a cultural study. Food is a super way to introduce children to another country, other traditions, or diverse cultures.
- Have students look for holiday-related recipes. The Thanksgiving Web site listed above is a good starting place for many different American holidays.
- Bind holiday recipes together into a class book.
- Students rewrite recipes in their own words.
- Collect all the recipes, make a copy for each student, and then make a cookbook for each student. With a personalized cover, this would make a nice Mother's Day gift.

WHAT'S COOKING? *(cont.)*

Recipe Card

Name_____   Serves_____

Recipe_____

Ingredients: _____

_____

_____

_____

Instructions: _____

_____

_____

_____

_____

_____

_____

GLOSSARY

America Online—one of the largest commercial online services in the world

Applications—synonym for computer programs

Archie—a computerized service on the Internet that helps find file transfer protocol (FTP) files

BBS—short for bulletin board service

Bits per Second (bps)—a measure of how quickly data can be sent

Bookmarks—URLs saved in a file for easy access

Browser—software used for looking at the Internet and World Wide Web

Call for Collaboration—a means of requesting other participants to join you in completing a project (See Global Schoolhouse for more.)

Chat—to talk to others via a computer

Client—a computer program that asks for some kind of data (file, software) from another computer (called a server)

Compressed—data that is squeezed together

CompuServe—along with Prodigy and America Online, one of the largest commercial online services in the world

Cyberspace—a general term given to the universe of computer communications

Data—information entered into a computer

Dedicated Line—a phone line set aside exclusively for one purpose

Dial-in Direct—one kind of Internet connection (Point-to-point protocol (PPP) and serial-line-interface protocol (SLIP) are the two main types of dial-in direct connections.)

Download—to transfer data (usually text, software, or graphics) from a remote (distant) computer to your computer

E-mail—short for electronic mail

Emoticons—human expressions created from keyboard characters (They help compensate for a reader's difficulty in interpreting emotion in printed text.)

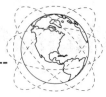

FAQ—short for frequently asked questions

Freeware—free software programs

FTP (File Transfer Protocol)—a commonly used means of moving large files across the Internet

Gopher—created at the University of Minnesota (home of the Golden Gophers), a browser-type service that allows menus to dig through information en route to a desired destination

Home Page—the first screen viewed when visiting a Web site

Host—a computer with which you connect and interact

HTML (HyperText Markup Language)—coding used to create hypertext documents and Web pages

Hypertext—a document form that features links to other documents in the form of graphics, text, sound, and movies

HTTP (HyperText Transport Protocol)—the most important protocol on the Web (This protocol allows for the movement of hypertext files across the Internet.)

Internet—a worldwide network of computer networks which, to name just three capabilities, offer data-sharing, electronic messaging, and online commerce

Log Off—to disconnect from another computer

Log On—to connect to an Internet provider, commercial online service, or other computer network

Megabyte—an amount of memory (1,024 kilobytes) needed to save a document of approximately 620 pages of double-spaced text

Modem—the device that uses phone lines or some other form of cable (fiber optic, ISDN) to connect your computer to distant computers

Netiquette—short for "network etiquette," stands for acceptable conduct in network communications

Newsgroups—not so much news groups as they are subject-oriented discussion groups where subscribers exchange opinions as much as they do facts

Newsreader—a software program for navigating through (i.e., select or ignore) the latest postings in the newsgroups to which you have subscribed

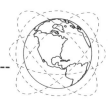

Offline—not connected to a computer network

Online—connected to a computer network

Posting—the act of submitting input to a computer bulletin board, newsgroup, or mailing list

PPP—see *dial-in direct*

Prodigy—financially owned by Sears and IBM, one of the three largest commercial online services in the world

Protocol—a proper way of doing things (in our context) by the software used for Internet connections

Server—a computer that offers services or functions to other computers (clients)

Service Provider—the label given to the organization (usually commercial) that offers Internet access

Shareware—try-before-you-buy software

SLIP—see *dial-in direct*

TCP/IP (Transmission Control Protocol/Internet Protocol)—protocol which defines the Internet (Your browser must have this software for you to be on the Internet.)

Telnet—a service available on the Internet that allows a user to connect to, navigate around, and glean resources (files, documents) from a remote computer

Upload—the opposite of download; to contribute a file electronically, usually for others' use

URL—short for uniform resource locator (This is the fancy name for a World Wide Web site's address.)

Usenet—short for the Users Network, provides discussion forums which currently number over 15,000

Veronica—Very Easy Rodent-Oriented Net Indexed Computerized Archives, a tool that searches Gopher files for requested information

WAIS—short for Wide Area Information Server

World Wide Web (The Web, WWW, W3)—the corner of the Internet highlighted by the millions of hypertext documents that are easily accessible to users of browser software

ZIP—a term used for compressed files (When viewed online, these files are listed with the extension .zip.)

BIBLIOGRAPHY

Ackermann, Ernest. *Learning to Use the Internet—An Introduction with Examples and Exercises.* Franklin, Beedle & Associates, 1995.

Butler, Mark. *How to Use the Internet.* Ziff-Davis Press, 1994.

Clark, David. *Student's Guide to the Internet.* Alpha Books, 1995.

Crumlish, Christian. *The Internet Dictionary—The Essential to Netspeak.* Sbyex, Inc., 1995.

Dern, Daniel P. *The Internet Guide for New Users.* McGaw-Hill, Inc., 1994.

Eddings, Joshua. *How the Internet Works.* Ziff-Davis Press, 1994.

Ellsworth, Jill H. *Education on the Internet.* Sams Publishing, 1994.

Engst, Adam. *The Internet Starter Kit for Macintosh.* Hayden Books, 1994.

Fraase, Michael. *The Mac Internet Tour Guide—Cruising the Internet the Easy Way* and *The Windows Internet Tour Guide—Cruising the Internet the Easy Way.* Ventana Press, 1995.

Frazer, Deneen, Barbara Kurshan and Sara Armstrong. *Internet for Kids.* Sybex, Inc., 1995.

Hahn, Harley & Rick Stout. *The Internet Yellow Pages.* Osborne McGraw-Hill, Inc., 1995.

Harris, Judi. *Way of the Ferret—Finding and Using Educational Resources on the Internet.* ISTE, 1995.

Leshin, Cynthia B. *Internet Adventures—Step-by-Step Guide for Finding and Using Educational Resources.* XPLORA Publishing, 1995.

Levine, John R. & Carol Baroudi. *The Internet for Dummies.* IDG Books, Inc., 1993.

Marsh, Merle. *Everything You Need to Know (But Were Afraid to Ask Kids) About the Information Highway.* Computer Learning Foundation, 1995.

Miller, Elizabeth, B. *The Internet Resource Directory for K–12 Teachers and Librarians.* Libraries Unlimited, Inc., 1996.

Pederson, Ted & Francia Moss. *Internet for Kids! A Beginner's Guide for Surfing the Net.* Price Stern Sloan, Inc., 1995.

Pfaffenberger, Bryan. *World Wide Web Bible.* MIS:Press, 1995.

Polly, Jean Armour. *The Internet Kids Yellow Pages.* Osborne McGraw-Hill, Inc., 1996.

Sachs, David & Henry Stair. *Instant Internet with WebSurfer.* Prentice Hall, 1995.

Strudwick, Karen, John Spilker, and Jay Arney. *Internet for Parents.* Resolution Business Press, 1995.

Williams, Brad. *The Internet for Teachers.* IDG Books Worldwide, 1995.